Foreword

Every learner needs to acquire fluency in basic literacy and numeracy as part of the core skills necessary for learning in all areas of the curriculum. Information Technology (IT) is being used very widely for writing, but IT can help learners develop more than neat presentation through word processing. It can help pupils to explore and develop ideas, and communicate them more effectively. IT can also provide flexible environments for exploring concepts of numeracy, such as estimation and it allows investigation of 'what if' scenarios.

This book presents a collection of ideas on different ways in which IT has been used successfully in schools to help pupils to develop their skills in these areas. In the project upon which this publication is based, a large number of schools were nominated by IT advisers, curriculum organisations or other bodies, for imaginative and high quality use of IT in literacy or numeracy. A number of these schools were invited to submit descriptions and examples of their work, which form the basis for the material here.

Its approach follows on the successful NCET publication *IT Works* in which a number of statements about the educational applications of IT were discussed. We have followed the same approach, but have illustrated each statement with material from participating schools, colleges and other sources. We have followed the common convention of using 'he' for the learner and 'she' for the teacher.

We hope that the ideas in this book will be of use to all teachers, giving ideas of ways in which IT can support learners, particularly those who are having difficulties with literacy and numeracy, and will encourage teachers to develop ideas of their own.

The 23 statements about IT and literacy and numeracy have been developed through an extensive consultation with experts in the field. There is not space for exhaustive discussion on each topic, and many readers will immediately identify areas that we could have illustrated. Both the general discussion and the illustrations are primarily intended to stimulate interest in the reader. As in *IT Works* we have included further reading lists for those who wish to follow up the ideas.

Good literacy and numeracy skills are important in all aspects of the curriculum. The purpose of this book is to provide a collection of tried and tested ideas to help all teachers to see where IT can help their pupils in these essential skills. We are very grateful to the many teachers and pupils who have taken part in this project, as well as to the various experts who have given valuable advice.

I am particularly grateful to Chris Abbott, who has written the book from the material gathered during the project and has accommodated the different perspectives with skill and goodwill.

Tina Detheridge

3

Contents

Section 1

Thinking, Learning and Exploring Ideas

Section 2

Expressing and Presenting Ideas

1   Learners can use IT to communicate ideas

Information Technology offers many different ways in which learners can communicate their own ideas. It allows them to try out different things to see what happens and to investigate the effect of different choices. For example they can investigate how different types of presentation can affect the meaning; explore which different forms of writing are appropriate for the content; experiment with tenses in the telling of a story; explore whether a graph or pie chart is the most appropriate way of representing something; decide whether to present figures in tables or words. Most importantly, with IT, everything can be put back to how it was if the choices turn out to be inappropriate or undesirable.

Ideas that are formed in this way can then be communicated to others through the use of word-processed documents, supported by the production of graphics or spreadsheets, and even sent over long distances by using electronic mail.

Although IT has greatly increased communication possibilities for all learners, it has been particularly helpful for those people who have communication difficulties of some kind. If someone is unable to speak, various speaking devices are available which can be controlled by the user; other devices enable deaf people to use telephones or blind people to read from a computer screen. IT is increasingly seen as being as much about communication as it is about technology, and young learners are developing considerable expertise in using those communicative possibilities.

Both of the following case studies come from special schools, but each, in their different ways, illustrates a way of working with IT which has helped students to explore and communicate ideas.

A unit for students who are hearing-impaired at a comprehensive school in East Sussex used two different multimedia programs to help their students explore ideas and present them to others.

I used a dialogue program to help Darren organise a science assignment. In this program two characters on a series of screens have empty 'speech bubbles' into which their dialogue can be written. Darren found it amusing to play the role of a scientist while his teacher acted the part of a youngster asking him what to do. Darren worked enthusiastically on this. Discussing what to include in his story has helped him to sequence his ideas and we have looked at ways of making the text more interesting by avoiding repetition of phrases. He has now completed his assignment but continues to work with the program.

A page from the bubble dialogue

A small all-age special school in Manchester caters for children with impaired speech or language but who have no significant hearing loss or generalised learning difficulties. The school used talking books to support the development of literacy skills.

Our children have a wide range of speech and language impairments which profoundly affect their ability to learn. These difficulties affect the pupils' development of literacy skills to varying degrees. One child may have a high level of mechanical reading skills but great problems extracting meaning; another may have a good level of understanding but enormous problems acquiring even a basic sight vocabulary.

Writing a simple, readable and coherent story is a daunting task for speech- and language-impaired children because so many intellectual, linguistic and interpersonal demands are involved. Each group of three or four children listened to a talking book and then created one of their own. They wrote the story, drew pictures and finally recorded the sounds to go with it. Using multimedia, the children in our school were able to overcome some of these difficulties to produce attractive talking storybooks without tears. They were very proud of their achievements.

The use of multimedia had a number of advantages: the children were highly motivated, they felt they were writing for a purpose and the collaborative approach meant that they could support each other. They were also able to use their best levels of spoken language in a meaningful situation and could edit their work because they wanted it to look and sound better, not because it was wrong.

Recording speech for a talking book

Further reading

McMahon, H., and O'Neill, B.: 'A story about storying' in Montieth (Ed.): *Computers and Language*, Intellect Books 1993 ISBN 1 871516 27 7

An account of the development of Bubble Dialogue by the researchers who produced it. This account also includes transcripts of young children using IT to communicate their ideas.

McKeown, S., and Tweddle, S.: 'Writing to explore ideas' in *Writing and Learning with IT*, NCET 1994 ISBN 1 85379 272 1

This section of the book considers the many ways in which writers can use IT to explore ideas and is illustrated with many examples and case studies.

Papert, S.: 'Perestroika and epistemological politics' in Harel and Papert (Eds.): *Constructionism*, Ablex Publishing Corporation 1991 ISBN 0 89391 786 9

A challenging examination of the extent to which computers have, so far, been used imaginatively to help children explore ideas rather than simply to complete predetermined tasks.

Raban, B.: 'Using the "craft" knowledge of the teacher as a basis for curriculum development: a review of the National Writing Project in Berkshire' in *Cambridge Journal of Education*, Vol.20 No.1, Carfax Publishing 1990 ISSN 0305 764 X

Although this article does not discuss IT, it does cover writing in many contexts that will be helpful to the reader interested in the integration of IT into the writing process.

2 Learners can use multimedia to access information through the combination of sound, image, written word and movement

The combination of text with sound and pictures can make ideas more accessible. Each element of the multimedia text can reinforce the meaning and its multisensory nature can help many learners to understand ideas and information that might be too difficult to gather just through text.

Using a traditional encyclopaedia requires a range of skills which some learners may not possess. Even if they do find the necessary information, it is likely to be in the form of text or, at best, a picture. With multimedia information sources, it is no longer essential to follow the conventional process of using an Index, Contents Page or other structural device, although these paths will be available as alternatives. Clicking on a word, entering a search term or selecting from a range of pictures are all alternatives possible with these newer ways of providing information. Learners using these information tools can be provided with information which might include text, graphics, sound and moving video. Similarly, students who find reading difficult may find the multisensory nature of multimedia texts helps them in their reading.

Accessing information from multimedia texts demands different skills from traditional information handling. These skills are often much more easily adopted and developed by students. The deaf children at a West London school were able to read the talking books used by the rest of the class once extra information, in the form of animated signing, was provided.

Leila had come over from Israel and was spending a year at a school in the Midlands. She received Section 11 support for part of the week but was encouraged to be as independent as possible. She used the Dorling Kindersley *My First Incredible Amazing Dictionary* which has a thousand words illustrated with sound, pictures and animation. She could click on words and hear the text spoken aloud, listen to the pronunciation of words and see what the word meant. Her vocabulary grew quite quickly and she was able to listen to words in context.

Sound, text, pictures and animations reinforce the meanings

A junior school in Hounslow, West London has 75% of pupils using a language other than English, mostly Punjabi, at home. The school chose to investigate the use of talking books with the 13 deaf children who spend over half of their time integrated into mainstream classes there.

For children whose main language is signing, one of the problems associated with learning to read is the link between the signed and printed word. Books have been produced with pictures of hand signs, but without the associated movement many of the signs mean nothing to children. We decided to use an animation program to make some moving signs which could be used with a series of talking book programs.

We chose a book called *The Go-Kart* because it had a story which translated into clear and unambiguous signs. A character from some of the other reading books was chosen as the storyteller; he is someone that the children recognise and relate to easily. Running the program loads the talking book in the usual way, but a row of icons also appear, numbered to match each page. Clicking on one of these pages brings up a picture of a boy, who speaks and signs the relevant page.

The signed version of *The Go-Kart* was trialled in the school's Centre for the Deaf and the reaction was extremely positive – the children loved it! Deaf children rarely see sign language anywhere except with their friends, family and teachers. Seeing signing on the screen created very high levels of motivation to use the program.

Hello!

The animated character signs 'hello'

One pupil, seven year old James, was enthusiastic about the program from the outset. He could not recognise all the signing on the screen, but having had it signed in 3D he was able to recognise it and recall it when he next used the program. James' learning is characterised by a short attention span; on the first occasion that we used the program he worked on it for almost an hour at his request. The hearing children in the school have tremendous fun with the talking books; James and his deaf peers are now fully able to join in the fun.

Further reading

Scrimshaw, P.: 'Reading, writing and hypertext' in Scrimshaw (Ed.) *Language, Classrooms and Computers*, Routledge 1993
ISBN 0 415 08575 6

A description of the issues developers must bear in mind when producing multimedia texts, and an examination of other issues related to this area.

Bolter, J.D.: *Writing Space: the Computer, Hypertext and the History of Writing*, Lawrence Erlbaum Associates 1991
ISBN 0 8058 0428 5

An examination of the development of writing from what the author calls the 'late age of print' to a time when multimedia texts have become increasingly accepted as the norm.

Abbott, C.: *Reading IT: a Teacher's Guide to the use of Computers in Reading Activities*, Reading and Language Centre, University of Reading 1994
ISBN 0 7049 0882 4

A beginner's guide for primary school teachers which examines the issues involved in reading from the screen rather than from a book.

Buckingham, D.: *Changing Literacies: Media Education and Modern Culture*, Tufnell Press 1993
ISBN 1 872767 61 3

The author assesses the importance of media education in the lives of our children.

3 Learners at the emergent writing stage can use IT to develop their understanding of how writing works, and of the links between speech, reading and writing

Learners who are beginning to write are learning to see writing as communication; are beginning to recognise letters; to distinguish capitals from lower case and to see the need for spaces between words. A word processor, with its clear letters and spacing can help children understand how writing works.

A word processor may provide another method by which children in the early stages of literacy development can experiment with writing, putting print on paper and inventing words. This can influence the development of young children to become confident about their abilities and see themselves as writers. This will most successfully happen alongside, and not instead of, other kinds of writing exploration on paper with pens and pencils.

Some learners will find it easier to read back some of their own writing after using a word processor. Many young learners can recognise errors and omissions on a computer screen much more easily than in their own hand-written texts.

I am Dave   This is my   Video Diary

A special school in an urban area near Newcastle used video, scanning and digitising equipment to produce video diaries featuring students with severe learning difficulties. The students, who were of secondary school age, wanted to have aspects of their home life included in their diaries as well. With the help of parents, home visits were made and video was also used of students taking part in Duke of Edinburgh's Award activities. The work was planned to contribute to the school's multisensory approach to literacy.

We selected students at the very early stages of reading who all had severe learning difficulties and limited language ability. They had an understanding that print conveys meaning, basic though incomplete letter recognition and they understood that words are made up of letters. We intended to provide devices such as a

trackerball and touch screen so that students could input text. In fact, the group managed well using a standard mouse and inputting text from the keyboard, with a little help provided. Students watched the video recordings and selected the scenes they wanted to include; then they were shown how to drag digitised pictures on to a page and choose a background colour. A considerable amount of language work took place as students decided on the text for each page. Students were very keen to read their diaries both on the computer screen and when they were printed out; their readings were recorded and added to the diaries.

Post-activity testing showed that all the students made substantial gains in their sight vocabularies; this increase was often a dramatic one. All the students also increased their fluency. The students were excited and well-motivated throughout the project and all said that they found it fun. This clearly has benefits in developing self-esteem, which in turn supports reading development.

Further reading

Wheatley, V.: 'Word processing in the nursery' in *Developing English: Approaches with IT*, NATE 1993 ISBN 0 901291 33 1

The author describes the use of a multilingual word processor to help children make connections with their language environment and to experiment with their first language using IT.

McKeown, S., and Tweddle, S.: 'Becoming a writer' in *Writing and Learning with IT*, NCET 1994 ISBN 1 85379 272 1

Overlay keyboards, first language support and early proof-reading are among the issues discussed in this section of the book.

4 Learners can be helped to develop appropriate vocabulary and grammatical choices by the use of specific kinds of writing software

Access to a thesaurus, predictive word processor or other similar tool can help learners explore vocabulary and understand how language works and the rules that it usually follows. These utilities, although semi-intelligent, will never provide complete solutions to any query, and writers will be required to evaluate the appropriateness of each suggestion in context. It will focus attention onto their choices of vocabulary and grammatical construction.

Grammar or style checkers may be helpful in this area, although possibly more useful as a means of investigating language than they are for their original intended purpose. The problem is often with the message given to the writer; the error may well be one which the writer needs to be aware of, but most grammar checkers confuse the learner by using complex language to describe the error.

Let the camera of your mind's eye picture New York. A vast city, where Skyscrapers tower above the busy streets, in which people go about their own personal business in their own personal way. Pan right and zoom in on a particularly inconspicuous small building, surrounded by a small green patch of grass which has obviously been placed there during one of the many failed attempts to bring some wildlife to the city. Zoom in again towards a fairly dark unobtrusive window, inside which a notably inconspicuous man is preparing to play a guitar, in a quite ordinary fashion, which would have attracted no attention whatsoever. This man was currently engaged in the kind of experiment that the U.S. government would have paid millions to get their hands on, if they had only known about it.

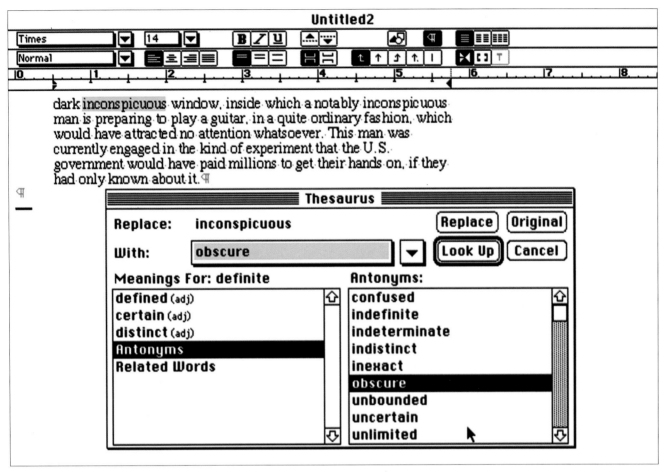

dark inconspicuous window, inside which a notably inconspicuous man is preparing to play a guitar, in a quite ordinary fashion, which would have attracted no attention whatsoever. This man was currently engaged in the kind of experiment that the U.S. government would have paid millions to get their hands on, if they had only known about it.

Thesaurus

Replace: inconspicuous

With: obscure

Meanings For: definite

defined (adj)
certain (adj)
distinct (adj)
Antonyms
Related Words

Antonyms:

confused
indefinite
indeterminate
indistinct
inexact
obscure
unbounded
uncertain
unlimited

A thesaurus can broaden vocabulary

Pupils in a secondary school in the Midlands used a word processor with thesaurus and a grammar checker to stimulate creative approaches to writing.

Paul, a Year 10 pupil, preparing coursework for GCSE, has been experimenting with language by using a thesaurus to give him ideas. In the example below, which already shows development on previous work, he was searching for an alternative to 'inconspicuous' which he had used three times.

```
a particularly inconspicuous
small building,

a fairly dark and
inconspicuous window

a notably inconspicuous man
```

He felt that three uses were too much, but thought the first right, and particularly liked the phrase 'notably inconspicuous'. He searched for an alternative to the second use – 'a dark and inconspicuous window'. The thesaurus gave first the alternative 'dim', which didn't suit his purpose, so he looked up antonyms for the related word 'conspicuous' – which led him to alternatives such as 'obscure', 'shadowy', 'hidden' 'unobtrusive' and 'barely discernible'. He chose to replace the phrase with 'a dark, unobtrusive window'.

Further reading

Williams, N.: 'Post writing software and the classroom' in Montieth (Ed.) *Computers and Language*, Intellect Books 1993
ISBN 1 871516 27 7

An analysis of various kinds of software proofing tools which comes to the conclusion that their potential is clear but that they currently fail to be as effective as teachers would wish.

Day, J.: 'Is good looking writing good writing?' in Singleton (Ed.): *Computers and Dyslexia*, Dyslexia Computer Resource Centre 1994
ISBN 1 898862 00 1

A description of the different kinds of software which may help at various stages in the writing process, with an emphasis on what IT can offer beyond spell checking and improvement in presentation.

5 Learners can use a spell checker to develop their own spelling strategies

Spell checkers can help pupils correct their own spelling mistakes, without being dependent upon the teacher for corrections. Small hand-held spell checkers can be particularly useful in providing help in any context.

Although a spell checker can be a useful tool, it is more useful to learners who need support than to those for whom spelling presents a major problem. Care should be taken by teachers to ensure that there is no over-reliance on their use. As with calculators, there will be a need to ask whether an answer makes sense in a given context, since most spell checkers look at words in isolation rather than considering them as they are being used. This means that homonyms, words which sound the same but are spelt differently, are not noticed by the spell checker: and neither are misspellings which happen to be the same as other words.

Despite these drawbacks, many learners find they benefit from the feedback provided during the checking process. Errors may form a pattern so that learners can internalise a rule from a series of corrections using the same group of letters, or they may notice other links between the words flagged by the computer. Some spell checkers offer extra facilities such as a thesaurus where the user can check for alternative words, or an in-built speech system which reads back the text. This is particularly useful for identifying repetitions or words which are grossly misspelt. The experiences of one ten year old girl are typical of the way in which strategies are developed by learners using IT.

Further reading

McKeown, S.: 'Microcomputer software: programs for writing and spelling' in *British Journal of Special Education*, Vol.19 No.3, National Association for Special Educational Needs 1992

  A description of spell checkers, their capabilities, and what they cannot be expected to do.

Hornsey, T.: 'Supporting reading and writing' in Singleton (Ed.): *Computers and Dyslexia*, Dyslexia Computer Resource Centre 1994
ISBN 1 898862 00 1

  A brief but clear overview of the ways in which IT can help learners with dyslexia.

McKeown, S. (Ed.): *IT Support for Specific Learning Difficulties*, NCET 1992
ISBN 1 85379 177 6

  A wide-ranging publication covering many issues related to IT and specific learning difficulties, this booklet also includes a detailed examination of various spell-checking programs and the differences between them.

An average sized urban primary school in the Midlands has one computer permanently sited in each classroom, which is used by the whole class for work across the curriculum. A Year 6 pupil with a severe spelling difficulty shared this for some of her writing.

Jane always enjoys art and practical work and she is good at Maths. However, she hates writing, and particularly dislikes spelling, which she finds very difficult. We found that providing her with a word processing program with a spell checker helped her a lot. Jane's problems with spelling have always been profound: she reverses letters like b and d or p, q and g and her phonic strategies have always been confused. As she has progressed through the school, Jane, who is now ten years old, has become very embarrassed about her difficulties. Her problems with spelling made her hate writing. She was encouraged by the use of a word processor, where she could correct the mistakes her teacher marked up. The introduction of a spell checker enabled her to correct mistakes without having to rewrite things. It allowed Jane to work in privacy and check her own writing. Soon, she found she was developing her own strategies for spelling and learning from her previous errors, which had been highlighted for her by the program. Jane has started to remember the spellings of many more words now. It has increased her independence and motivation to write.

A central Birmingham primary school which opened fairly recently and is well equipped with computers uses portables to support all pupils especially those with special needs.

One child worked with a special needs teacher to produce a well-presented, correctly spelt and punctuated piece of work. Pupils of all abilities have benefited from the use of the computers, and the support they provide for writing. The pupils made particular use of the spell checking facility and were able to develop their own strategies for selecting words and improving what they had written. Their comments make clear the value they found in using computers in this way:

"I like the spell check because I am bad at spellings."
"I also like the spell check because if we have got a word wrong or we have not put a space after a full stop, they will show it."
"It's got a spell check and that's better than going to your book and underlining it."

However, not everything about the computers met with approval; a message here for the manufacturers perhaps:

"I hate the colour because they are all black and it would be better if there were more colours."

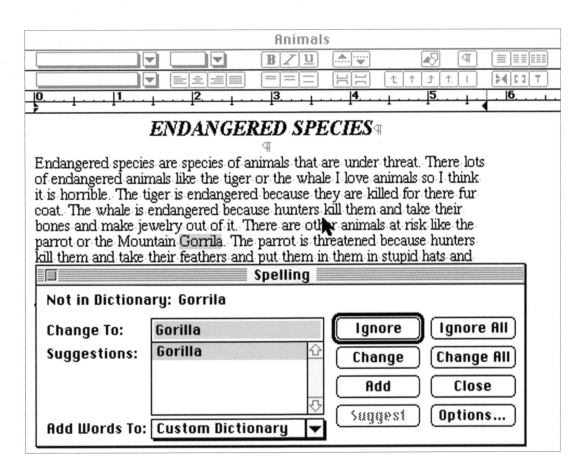

6 Learners can develop clearer mental images of numbers if they see them displayed in various ways on the computer screen

Learners need to construct mental images of numbers in order to handle numbers with ease and IT can help them to do this. Software can show numbers in many different ways: the number 6 can be replaced by six cars or six bees, arranged in regular patterns so that these visual images can be seen and remembered. IT can also be very useful in helping learners visualise very large or very small numbers by the display of number lines and number squares. Learners can develop their visual sense of numbers and the patterns they make by their use of these lines and squares. IT can help to make this learning dynamic and interactive.

Histograms, pie charts and other visual displays, which can be generated from numbers entered into a spreadsheet or database can help children 'see' relative sizes of number. Through the software the learner can see the same data displayed in different ways which will help in creating mental images.

Two examples given below show different ways in which IT has been used in this way.

Further reading

McKeown, S. (Ed.): *Dyslexia and Mathematics*, NCET 1993
ISBN 1 85379 246 2

> Many of the case studies in this book of ideas relate to the use of IT to understand numbers.

Kerslake, D., et al: 'Number patterns' in *Micromath*, Vol.10 No.1, ATM 1994

> Computers, and spreadsheets in particular, offer powerful ways of generating number patterns quickly. These and related issues are discussed in a series of articles.

Getting Started with Information Handling, NCET 1994
ISBN 1 85379 293 4

> A pack which takes the reader through the process of developing information handling skills.

Parker, J., and Widmer, C.C.: 'Teaching mathematics with technology: how big is a million?' in *Arithmetic Teacher*, Vol.39 No.1, pp.38–41, September 1991
ISSN: 0004 136 X

> Included are activities and guidelines which suggest ways to use large numbers in relative terms so that they become more meaningful for elementary mathematics students. Several spreadsheet projects illustrate the incorporation of the recommendations from the NCTM Standards dealing with number sense.

A large urban primary school in Southampton planned a programme of work on the topic of Toys. The Year 3 children involved were in two mixed ability classes, although for some mathematical work pupils worked on differentiated tasks in ability groups. IT featured strongly in the topic and was used by the teachers to plan activities and produce task sheets.

A small first school in South Dorset used Logo to help young pupils gain a feel for numbers. There are 130 pupils at the school, aged from 4 to 9 years. One group decided to use Logo to draw a bus.

We planned to use IT in many different ways in our Toys topic. In Mathematics this included generating worksheets on measurement, colour combinations and money, data handling and constructing pictograms. We also made floor plans of houses for a teddy bear.

Data displayed in various ways in a presentation package

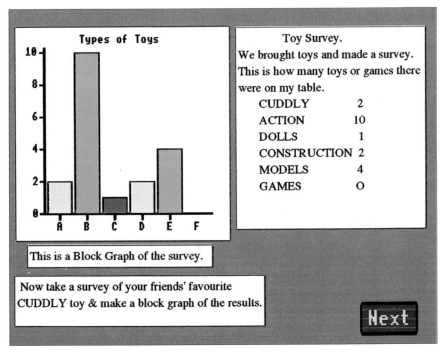

Types of Toys

This is a Block Graph of the survey.

Now take a survey of your friends' favourite CUDDLY toy & make a block graph of the results.

Toy Survey.
We brought toys and made a survey. This is how many toys or games there were on my table.

CUDDLY	2
ACTION	10
DOLLS	1
CONSTRUCTION	2
MODELS	4
GAMES	O

Next

Designing and making these teddy bear houses involved introducing children to the idea of scale. We gave the children a teddy of suitable size for the boxes we had; each group chose a different room to make. We also asked the children to complete a survey of the different kinds of toys they own; they entered the results into the computer and displayed this as a graph.

The children drew a rough sketch of a bus and then they started to work out the length of each line. They were not sure how far FORWARD 1 was, so they decided to check that first using the floor turtle. They checked FORWARD 100 as well and then worked out what instructions they would need to give the floor turtle. They entered their instructions into the computer as a procedure and watched the turtle draw their picture. It seemed to start off OK and then they laughed as it drew something they had not expected. They decided to try a second bus. They looked back over their program to see if they could work out where they went wrong:

Vicky: If that was 6 last time then I think it should be about 10. Then it's RT 90.
Lucy: If that's 100 then it's probably FD about 150.
Vicky: Then LT 90.
Lucy: FD again.
Vicky: From there to there was 350 so this must be about 100 less.

Bus 2 came out to their expectations and, although their calculations were not always completely accurate, it was interesting to see how quickly they were able to build upon their experiences from their first design. Their second design generated lots more mathematical discussion and they seemed more able to visualise the distances.

7 Learners can use computers and calculators to produce many examples, to explore patterns and to make generalisations

The speed of computers and calculators enables students to produce many examples when exploring mathematical problems. This can support their observation of patterns. As the patterns build up on the screen learners are often able not only to see the pattern that is forming, but also to explain why. A particular pattern can be recorded and analysed, enabling the learner to predict its progression.

Both calculators and computer programs that manipulate numbers can, by simplifying the procedures, help children find the answers to calculations without having to go through lengthy procedures. As well as speeding up the process, calculators help learners to produce reliable results. Imagine children, uncertain of their mathematics, multiplying numbers without a calculator, taking the entire lesson to complete six calculations and getting two of the six wrong! There is no possibility that these children could discover a pattern.

Further reading

Hawkridge, D., and Vincent, T.: *Learning Difficulties and Computers*, Jessica Kingsley Publishers 1992
ISBN 1 85302 132 6

Chapter 10: Number and Mathematical Reasoning describes this work with turtles and repeating number patterns, plus mosaics and overlay keyboards.

McKeown, S. (Ed.): *Dyslexia and Mathematics*, NCET 1993
ISBN 1 85379 246 2

Some of the 'early years' case studies in this book of ideas relate to the use of IT to investigate patterns.

Battista, M.: 'Research into practice: calculators and computers: tools for mathematical exploration and empowerment' in *Arithmetic Teacher*, Vol.41 No.7, 1994
ISSN 0004 136 X

This article discusses ways that calculators and computer microworlds, such as Logo, can be used as tools for exploration, problem-solving, and empowerment in school mathematics. The article includes suggestions for classroom activities.

A secondary school for pupils with emotional and behavioural difficulties in the South East used a turtle graphics program to motivate pupils to explore number patterns.

At a school in Hertfordshire for boys with emotional and behavioural difficulties, IT is used to motivate pupils and as a tool for investigation. In this example pupils used a turtle graphics program to promote the development of mathematical skills.

The boys were asked to make observations, comparisons and deductions based on the times tables. The emphasis on the relationship between the sets of numbers helped to promote greater understanding. The program was used to explore the relationships contained in sets of numbers. By expressing these as shapes and patterns on the computer screen, a concrete, and thus more meaningful, representation could be obtained. This would have been too daunting a task, and difficult to achieve with accuracy by hand.

The investigation is based on the fact that each times table can be reduced by adding the digits in the table together to produce single digit numbers which form a repeating pattern (Fig 1). When the repeating number patterns are plotted as lengths with a right angled turn between each length then a line pattern emerges (Fig 2). The computer was used to plot them. When the line pattern was repeated with a right angled turn after each repeat it was found that after four repeats it returns to its point of origin, producing a distinctive pattern (Fig 3).

Mark, a 10 year old boy, approached the investigation enthusiastically. Each pattern produced was printed out and stuck onto card so that they could be observed together. Having produced patterns derived from the complete set of tables, Mark wanted to extend the investigation. The investigation extended Mark's mathematical understanding and provided him with an enjoyable experience which enhanced his self-esteem For pupils like Mark such opportunities are of tremendous value.

Patterns made from number sequences

4 times table	Reduction of the table	Repeating number pattern
1 x 4 = 4	4 + 0 = 4	4
2 x 4 = 8	8 + 0 = 8	8
3 x 4 = 12	1 + 2 = 3	3
4 x 4 = 16	1 + 6 = 7	7
5 x 4 = 20	2 + 0 = 2	2
6 x 4 = 24	2 + 4 = 6	6
7 x 4 = 28	2 + 8 = 10 = 1 + 0 = 1	1
8 x 4 = 32	3 + 2 = 5	5
9 x 4 = 36	3 + 6 = 9	9
10 x 4 = 40	4 + 0 = 4	4
11 x 4 = 44	4 + 4 = 8	8
12 x 4 = 48	4 + 8 = 12 = 1 + 2 = 3	3
etc.	etc.	etc

Fig. 1

```
4X
FORWARD 40
RIGHT 90
FORWARD 80
RIGHT 90
FORWARD 30
RIGHT 90
FORWARD 70
RIGHT 90
FORWARD 20
RIGHT 90
FORWARD 60
RIGHT 90
FORWARD 10
RIGHT 90
FORWARD 50
RIGHT 90
FORWARD 50
RIGHT 90
FORWARD 90
RIGHT 90
```

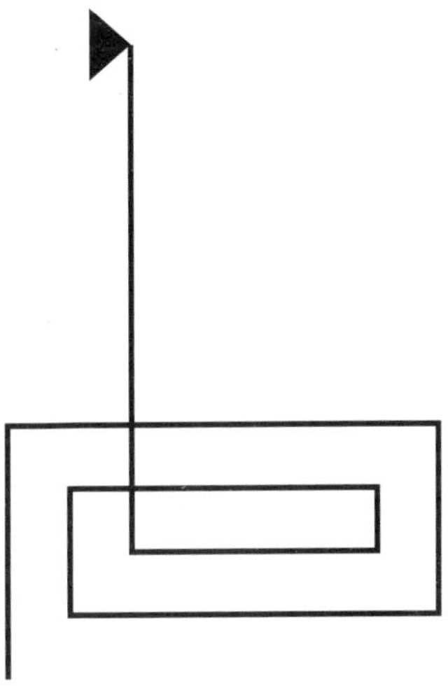

Fig. 2

```
4XPAT

REPEAT 4
  4X
END
```

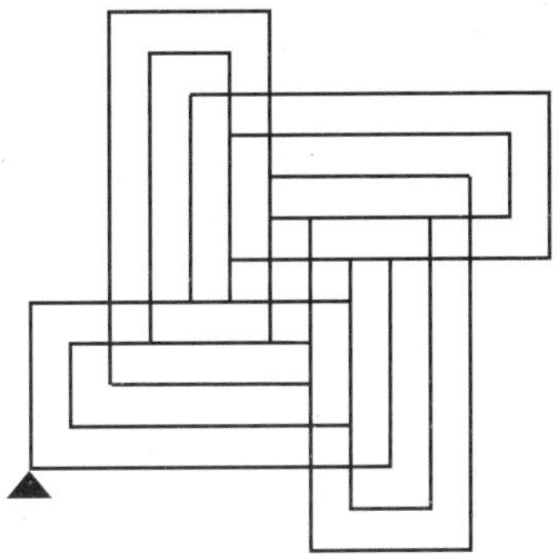

Fig. 3

8 Learners developing an understanding of place value can be helped by talking calculators

Place value can be a difficult concept for many learners. Numbers which contain the same digits in different orders are often confused. Confusions between numbers such as 110, 101 and 1001 can be diminished by hearing those numbers spoken and displayed by a talking calculator; this support can be used for as long as is needed, then occasionally invoked for checking, and eventually no longer used when the learner is able to recognise numbers confidently. Similarly, hearing decimal numbers spoken can help to clarify numbers. Some dyslexic pupils have particular difficulty with digit order; for example, they may write 132 for 'one hundred and twenty three'. Hearing the numbers spoken will draw their attention to any differences between the digits they have actually entered and the number required.

Calculators can do more than provide answers

An adult basic education unit in Coventry with a large number of woman returners and unemployed adults who were keen to improve their numeracy skills decided to use calculators, including talking calculators, to help students work more independently.

We found that some of our students had problems writing numbers down or remembering them. Many had problems with short term memory so that they could not remember a number with more than two or three digits. They would get 5382, for example, confused with 5832 or even 8352. We hoped that the use of a talking calculator would overcome some of these problems because it would allow students to hear what they had just entered.

Melanie always wrote numbers like 304 when she should be writing 34: she was simply writing the 'thirty' first and then adding the 'four'. When she used a talking calculator it read out 'three hundred and four' when she was expecting it to say 'thirty-four'. This allowed her to check her work and she was soon able to correct the numbers which she entered wrongly. After a while, she was able to do this without using the speech from the calculator.

We found that the talking calculator also helped those students who had problems differentiating between the different symbols: '+' and 'x' look very similar but they sound very different. We were particularly interested to discover that the aural feedback provided by listening to mathematical operations being spoken aloud definitely helped students who have problems with number bonds and tables. The speech provided by the calculator made the learning process auditory as well as visual and tactile, enabling a multisensory approach.

A physics class in an inner city school in North London.
A 12 year old boy with learning difficulties has difficulty with the mathematics involved.

During a physics activity Matthew had to multiply 2.5 by 12. He did this by adding up 2.5 twelve times and came to the answer 'twenty four point sixty' (24.60) Clearly he had no realisation of place value at all. His teacher gave him a talking calculator to help him, which correctly pronounced the figures after the decimal point, which helped him realise that the numbers either side of the decimal point were not entirely independent. Repeatedly adding 2.5 and seeing the answer grow helped him to understand the approach.

Further reading

Duffin, J. et al: 'Calculators' in *Micromath*, Vol.8 No. 1, ATM 1992

> Janet Duffin and others write extensively about calculators in this group of articles. Although talking calculators are not explicitly included, there is much here that will inform their use.

McKeown, S. (Ed.): *Dyslexia and Mathematics*, NCET 1993
ISBN 1 85379 246 2

> Some of the 'early years' case studies in this book of ideas relate to the use of IT to investigate patterns.

Schielack, J.: 'Reaching young pupils with technology' in *Arithmetic Teacher*, February 1991, pp 51–55

> Discusses the use of computers and calculators with kindergarten and primary school pupils. Concludes that IT can enhance all pupils' opportunities to explore mathematical concepts, to generate patterns, to make conjectures about their patterns and to test their conjectures.

9 Learners can develop their expertise at estimation by using a range of IT tools

Robots can be very helpful, especially for young learners who are just beginning to appreciate the comparative values of numbers. These popular devices are immediately accessible to young learners. They are inexpensive and capable of a wide range of uses. Learners can be asked to predict, estimate or measure the distance travelled by a floor robot, and can record and assess their growing ability to estimate.

The use of floor turtles and Logo can also assist in this area, and can be planned as a progression from programming robots. Learners need to estimate distances travelled and angles turned when purposefully manipulating a floor turtle. Furthermore, after each estimate, the turtle actions will give an immediate feedback on the accuracy of the prediction.

The drawing of turtle graphics on screen using Logo is a logical progression from programming a turtle, and pupils who have completed one activity successfully will be able to move confidently to the other.

Using turtles to check estimates of distance

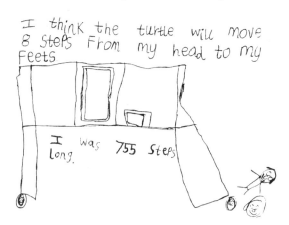

Case Study B

Six and seven year old children estimated how tall they thought they would be in 'turtle' steps. They could, if wished, check how far one turtle step was before making their estimation. Some children guessed wildly:

I think the turtle will move 8 steps from my head to my feets

I was 755 steps long.

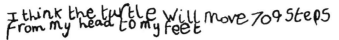

Others were able to make more calculated estimates:

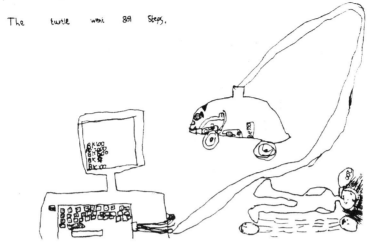

I think the turtle will move 709 steps
From my head to my feet

The turtle went 89 steps.

A first school class of six and seven year olds in Dorset tried to estimate their height and the length of the school corridor. Other children in the school used a floor robot and a number line to investigate distances and relationships between numbers, and to estimate how far the floor robot should move along a number line.

The children could, if they wished, check how far one turtle step was before making their estimation. Some children guessed wildly; others were able to make more calculated estimates. The children's estimates became increasingly more accurate as more people were measured. Then, one six year old estimated and measured the length of the corridor using a floor robot. When the robot stopped after 30 steps they were able to re-calculate the distance. Anne takes up the story. "First of all I thought it was 100. Jane thought it was 30 steps. We tried 30, I thought it was halfway there. So we pressed another 30. We were near the door. I pressed 6. We went a bit in the classroom. Altogether it was 66 steps."

Children can benefit from using Logo because they can see instantaneously what they have drawn and whether something is as they had intended it to be. Logo helps children to relate their ideas and concepts into real lines or movement, giving them a reason and a sense of purpose. By working in groups the children were able to communicate their mathematical ideas and discuss what they thought should happen.

Further reading

Hawkridge, D., and Vincent, T.: *Learning Difficulties and Computers*, Jessica Kingsley Publishers 1992 ISBN 1 85302 132 6

Chapter 2: 'Learners with cognitive difficulties' describes the use of Logo and maze programs at a special school.

Rose, S.: 'Learning through Logo' in *Micromath*, Vol.9 No.1, ATM 1993

This article describes the way in which a Year 3 class used Logo and a floor turtle.

Cannon, M.: 'Turtle games' in *Micromath*, Vol.10 No.2, ATM 1994

A description of the use of a floor turtle and Logo with seven- and eight-year-old primary pupils.

10 Learners writing collaboratively are helped by using IT

Writing collaboratively can be much easier sitting around a computer screen than it is when the participants are sharing a piece of paper, as many teachers have found when writing a joint school policy on an area of the curriculum. What has been written on a computer screen is much more likely to be viewed as a genuinely collaborative product, unlike a written text which will inevitably be more clearly owned by the member of the group who did the writing. The collaboration can be over a single piece of writing produced by discussion between a group, or can be a compilation of individual work, as in a class newspaper.

The use of electronic mail or video links enables collaboration across much greater distances and with many and varied groups of people. Writing can be begun by one group of children in one country and finished by another group elsewhere; or teachers working on common areas can exchange and edit each other's plans.

```
once upon a time there was a cat
called scruffy he lived in a hole in
a garden wall he went to look for
food he had to look in the most
unusual places he looked in dustbins
and sometimes he sat outside the
fishshop waiting for a treat his
favorite fish was kippers because he
would sit on the wall and spit the
bones out at all the dogs that walked
passed they couldnt get him up on the
wall so they would bark untill the
man from the fishshop came and
shouted at them to go away then
scruffy would jump down and go home
```

A collaborative story by a parent and child

> A group of Year 10 pupils used a collaborative writing approach to produce a script for a drama production.

Initially the group planned the shape of the piece, agreed the storyline and characters, then each pupil took on their character role to develop. Although each participant was responsible for one character, a great deal of negotiation and collaboration was required throughout the process. The final piece had a lot of variety, each part in the play had a very different character, and each participant was equally involved in the whole production as a result of the collaboration.

> An infant school in Newham, East London, set up a weekly workshop for parents and children to work together. The school has high mobility and serves a large number of different ethnic minority groups. About 70% of the pupils are bilingual, although many do not speak English when they first enter the school.

We feel as a school that we do not always have enough time to sit with pupils and support them in their use of IT. We came up with the idea of using our parents, who have always been very supportive in the past. Parents attended a workshop every Monday morning; we had to limit the session to six Mums because of our limited number of computers. The first session was for adults only to develop confidence, but later sessions all involved children working collaboratively.

Although the original aim of the project was to work towards the children developing their information retrieval strategies alongside the parents, this was possibly over-ambitious. It is hoped that the Mums will next term go into other classrooms and work with different children; three have agreed to do this. It was unfortunate that out of the twelve pupils involved, only two were girls. One of the local schools heard about what we were doing and came along to one of the sessions to have a look. They now hope to set up a similar scheme in their own school.

Further reading

Groundwater-Smith, S.: 'Beyond the individual: collaborative writing and the microcomputer' in Montieth (Ed.): *Computers and Language,* Intellect Books 1993
ISBN 1 871516 27 7

   The author describes collaborative writing among a group of secondary-aged students linked through electronic mail with their counterparts in other countries.

Light, P.: 'Collaborative learning with computers' in Scrimshaw (Ed.) *Language, Classrooms and Computers,* Routledge 1993
ISBN 0 415 08575 6

   A description of the ways in which computers can support not just writing but collaborative learning of many different kinds.

Scrimshaw, P.: 'Co-operative writing with computers' in Scrimshaw (Ed.) *Language, Classrooms and Computers,* Routledge 1993
ISBN 0 415 08575 6

   This chapter looks at a number of classroom activities involving collaborative writing and then underlines the importance of the scaffolding provided by the teacher in each case.

Karen's poems in Bain, R., Fitzgerald, B., and Taylor, M. (Eds.): *Looking into Language,* Hodder & Stoughton

11 Learners can use overlay keyboards or on-screen equivalents such as word banks to write phrases and key words with a single press

Paper grids on overlay keyboards, or on-screen grids and word banks, can provide support to readers for whom the typing of texts is a time-consuming or difficult task. Very early writers and learners with some degree of motor impairment can be helped to surmount these difficulties, to some degree, by the use of these devices. A word list can present new or difficult words and enable the student who can recognise but not spell certain key words to write fluently, without having to stop to search. Other lists may act in the way an older pupil might use a thesaurus, by offering alternatives and more adventurous vocabulary than the pupil may conjure up immediately.

There is a wide range of resources available to give this type of support to the learner. Some are in the form of resource packs, but the improved quality of utilities by which teachers can configure keyboard overlays, and more recently, grids that appear on screen, make this a realistic option for teachers to provide support for individuals or groups.

It is important to ensure that, where possible, the provision of word banks or pre-determined overlays does not constrain the writer or force the use of words that may not be entirely appropriate or which may not be the ones he wanted. This can be avoided by partial rather than complete use of a word bank, the availability of a wide and changing range of overlays and access to a teacher or other adult when needed. The most successful compilations of words for word banks are likely to be those the children have been involved in creating.

A description of work at an FE College and at a middle school demonstrates the wide age-range of students who can be helped in this way.

Further reading

McKeown, S.: 'Adult learners with reading difficulties' in Singleton (Ed.): *Computers and Dyslexia*, Dyslexia Computer Resource Centre 1994
ISBN 1 898862 00 1

A description of the kinds of support IT can provide for adult learners, particularly through the use of word banks and overlay keyboards.

Rahamim, L.: *Access to Words and Images*, NCET/CENMAC 1993 ISBN 1 85379 251 9

This publication looks at the ways in which IT can support the learning of students with physical disabilities. It contains many examples of the use of overlay keyboards, switches and specialised software.

Hawkridge, D., and Vincent, T.: *Learning Difficulties and Computers*, Jessica Kingsley Publishers 1992
ISBN 1 85302 132 6

Chapter 7: 'Reading' describes work with overlay keyboards which, although mostly directed towards reading support, has much to offer those developing writing resources.

Microscope, Spring 1995 (Concept Keyboard special)

Contains a wealth of ideas about using overlay keyboards, including several on basic mathematical understanding.

With the help of the local IT Centre, further education students in Humberside used overlay keyboards during their NVQ Catering and Hospitality course.

There is a great deal of specialised vocabulary used in catering and many of the overlays produced were linked to this need. Other overlays were related to matching exercises, so that terms such as 'à la carte' or 'table d'hôte' could be matched to the correct definition. Some overlays were pictorial, and students were required to name the vegetables and other ingredients shown on them. Students also needed to recognise safety signs on equipment, and overlays were produced to deal with this area. Sequencing activities were used on overlays dealing with the stages of meal preparation and recipes.

A middle school in Derbyshire uses many strategies to help their pupils.

Andrew's class have been using a word processor which allows many different kinds of writing support to be provided. He writes in blue text on a yellow background as he finds that combination is easier to read over a long period. The program also offers a word bank, and we have created a list there of all the words that Andrew finds difficult to spell. He copies these words from the word bank as he needs them, and this helps to fix them in his mind. We have given him another list of words for our class History topic, the Tudors. He can easily get access to words like 'Elizabeth', 'Sir Francis Drake' or 'beheaded', and he inserts these by clicking on them. There would be no benefit in asking Andrew to copy type these words as he is unlikely to need to spell them at this stage, although he does need to be able to use them. As the word processor he is using also offers the facility to speak any of the words, Andrew can listen to any of them if he is unable to read them.

An on-screen grid, as an alternative to an overlay keyboard

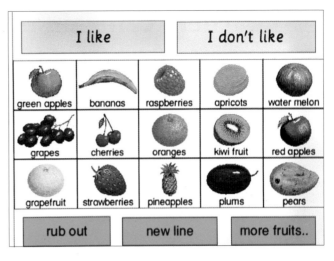

Writing using a word bank

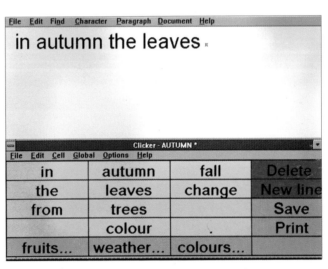

A keyboard overlay for catering students

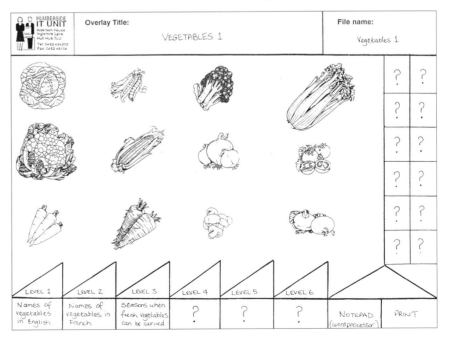

27

12 Learners can gain privacy and a feeling of security when writing with computers

The extra support which computers can provide can also be a source of privacy to writers who would otherwise require the assistance of another person. Learners with physical disabilities who are unable to speak can use electronic communication aids to prepare and deliver to others their thoughts and wishes. They are also able to access electronic mail and other communication systems, so that through the use of IT they are able to contact their friends and colleagues in confidence.

Students with emotional difficulties have been found to regard computer-based writing as less personal. They have been seen to share their work and accept criticism or comment of work printed out much more easily than remarks made about handwritten work. The computer seems to confer a kind of objectivity to their creation.

Writing software also helps learners who can only work slowly by enabling them to be confident about their ability to store accurately what they have written. It is, of course, essential that teachers ensure that back-ups are systematically taken in such cases so that this trust in the technology is not misplaced. A Birmingham primary school found that portable computers were very popular with pupils particularly because of the privacy and security they offered.

A pupil working at home

A primary school in central Birmingham used 24 portable computers to support a class of 30 Year 6 pupils. Pupils had access to the computers for several sessions each week. After some training in how to use the portables, the children used them mostly for creative writing. The school plans to use the portables in other lessons in future, including science, history and religious education.

Some of the students worked very slowly at the beginning, but after one or two sessions they were producing work much more quickly. The portable computers have provided pupils with an accessible and user-friendly tool to draft writing and to complement the school's desktop computers. Pupils from a broad range of abilities have from the beginning worked independently: accessing, formatting, loading and retrieving work from their own personal discs, and finding the convenience, portability and size of the portables a real bonus. The comments of two Year 6 girls speak for themselves:

"It is fun because if we are writing a story or something private nobody can look. I don't dislike anything apart from people coming and looking at my password."

"I like the laptops because it's got a password and that's better than the big computer."

Primary pupils using portable computers

Further reading

Stradling, B., Sims, D., and Jamison, J.: *Portable Computers Pilot Evaluation Summary,* NCET 1994
ISBN 1 85379 301 9

Portable computers offer considerable opportunities for private working and a feeling of security. This project report lists the other gains of working with small, portable computers.

Howard, B.: *IT Across the Curriculum: Supporting Learners who Display Challenging Behaviour,* NCET 1991

This discusses the way that IT can provide a feeling of security in writing. Although the work cited did not take place using portables, the issues are appropriate and the article covers the same issues of privacy.

13 Learners (and their teachers) can use IT to keep a continuous record of individual progress, which can be used to inform teaching and learning

It is very easy to keep records of work produced on a computer. Successive drafts of a piece of writing can be dated to demonstrate the growth of the ideas. Some programs will automatically date files, which is particularly helpful. Reflection on the changing work will help both student and teacher to see development, to gain a feeling of progress and to highlight recurring difficulties.

Integrated management or learning systems attempt to track progress across a range of activities within a suite of programs or when using other IT materials. Some of these systems contain diagnostic elements which can provide teachers with feedback so that they can become informed about the progress made by the user. Individual progress is measured and in many cases, appropriate next tasks are allocated. Learners can also use these features to inform themselves about their own progress. It is important that this feedback is provided in a form which is useful to the user, and gives clear guidance as to steps which need to be taken to address areas of difficulty. There is considerable interest in this area and more needs to be known about the kinds of learning that can be supported in this way.

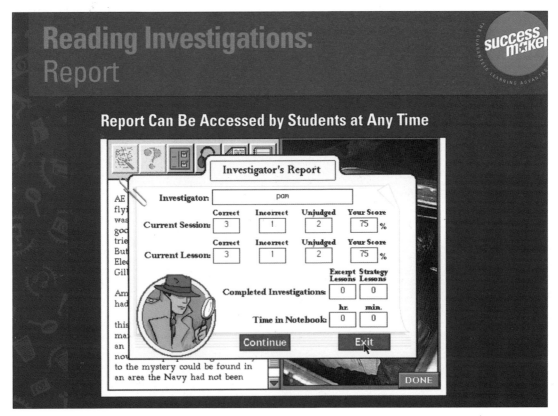

A student report from a computer activity

A large city secondary school in an urban area used the reading module of an Integrated Learning System.

We were using an integrated learning system with a Year 8 class. The Reading Investigations module asked children to read a piece of text in short sections. After each section they were asked to answer some questions in order to check that they had been reading carefully. The software showed the children how to approach these questions by looking for the answers in the text. The first questions were very simple and direct, but once success had been achieved with these, the emphasis shifted to comprehension of the text. The children were also asked to predict what they thought would happen next.

The children liked this way of working as they valued the immediate feedback provided; they also enjoyed being able to work at their own pace, without waiting for a teacher to check what they had done or help them out with difficulties.

Lindy, a rather shy girl in the class, particularly enjoyed being told by the software that she had learned to answer questions effectively. We feel that the program helped Lindy to work

at her own pace, and her teacher found that the detailed reports produced by the software helped him to understand the gradual progress being made, so that he could respond positively to this. Of course, he recognised that Lindy's usual reluctance to make oral contributions would not be improved by the software, but he did feel that her increase in confidence was noticeable and that she was beginning to be more adventurous in her creative writing.

Pupils using an integrated learning system

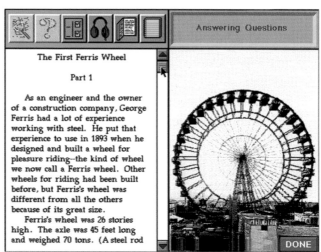

Further reading

Integrated Learning Systems: a report of the pilot evaluation of ILS in the UK, NCET 1994
ISBN 1 85379 310 8

> A report published by NCET and based on the full evaluation of the ILS pilot carried out by the University of Leicester.

Singleton, C., and Thomas, K.: 'Computerised screening for dyslexia' in Singleton (Ed.): *Computers and Dyslexia*, Dyslexia Computer Resource Centre 1994
ISBN 1 898862 00 1

> A description of research in this area and of the development of the dyslexia early screening test produced by the Dyslexia Resource Centre at the University of Hull.

Using IT for Assessment: Going Forward and *Directory of Software*, NCET 1994
ISBN 1 85379 294 2/1 85379 287 X

> The results of a survey carried out by NCET in 1993/1994 into the range of software available for recording and assessment by teachers, and some guidance in dealing with this area.

Tweddle, S.: 'Developing Tray as an assessment tool' in *Developing English: Approaches with IT*, NATE 1993
ISBN 0 901291 33 1

> A description of how the scratchpad feature in this popular program can be used to assist teacher assessment and student self-assessment.

14 Learners can be helped to move from concrete to abstract representations of number by their use of IT

Many learners can manipulate numbers with confidence when they have concrete objects to handle; when they transfer to using written numbers to represent those concepts they frequently meet some difficulty. The use of specially-designed software can assist in this transition process, and there is a wide range of such software available, especially for learners with special educational needs.

Astute teachers will ensure that further links are added between the objects represented on screen and their counterparts available in concrete form. If a program shows pictures of pigs on the screen, having copies of those pictures on the desk to be handled can help the transition process. Eventually, the manipulation of these objects will take place on the screen, and then by representation in numerical form.

There are students who for a variety of reasons may not have grasped some of the basic mathematical understandings that are normally gained through playing with concrete objects. For example, a pupil with a physical disability with limited motor capability may not have used puzzles and shapes to sort and manipulate in pre-school activities. Some students who do not have English as their first language may find revision of basic concepts valuable in making one-to-one correspondence between objects or between groups of items and their numerical representation. Some of the basic manipulative activities and games that can be carried out on computers can provide many opportunities to reinforce these basic concepts by simplifying the physical or cognitive process involved.

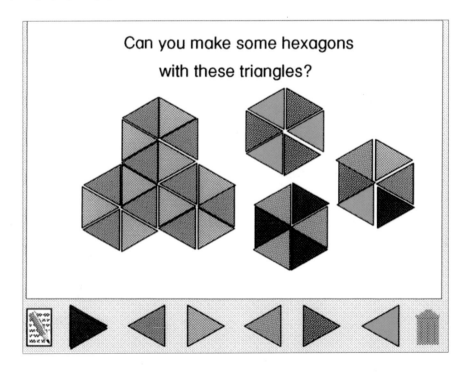

Many pupils in a junior class of a special school have physical disabilities.

Most of the pupils in this class have physical disabilities which have prevented them engaging in many of the play activities that very young children engage in at the pre-school stage. For this reason, James had difficulty understanding number. He had not gained a feel for the physical quantities of number and quantity through concrete experience. James could not use a standard keyboard because of his very restricted movement, but he could use a trackerball with a handrest instead of a mouse.

Using a program which had objects on the screen that he could move with a pointer, James built towers, and played with numbers of shapes, grouping them, matching them and counting them. This gave him access to the concrete experiences he had missed. Introduction of alternative representations, through domino dots and numerals, enabled him to directly make the links between quantity and its representation.

Liam, in the same class, used other software to explore mazes to help his understanding of space and direction.

Much of this type of software can be used through a range of input devices such as a touch screen, overlay keyboard, or even switches as well as trackerball and the standard keyboard.

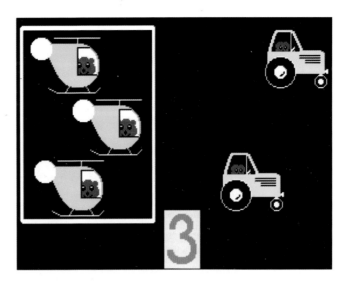

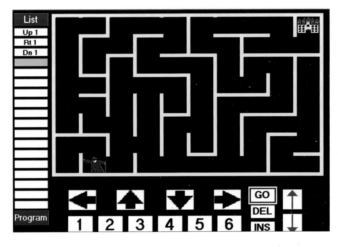

Software that can be used by pupils who cannot use a keyboard

Further reading

Clayton, P.: 'Using computers for numeracy and mathematics with dyslexic students' in Singleton (Ed.): *Computers and Dyslexia*, Dyslexia Computer Resource Centre 1994
ISBN 1 898862 00 1

  A summary of the areas of numeracy where IT can support learners, and a description of some of the software which the author has found to be useful.

McKeown, S. (Ed.): *Dyslexia and Mathematics*, NCET 1993
ISBN 1 85379 246 2

  Some of the 'early years' case studies in this book of ideas relate to the use of IT to move from concrete to abstract representation.

Sewell, D.F.: 'The release of cognitive resources – What can the enabling technology achieve?' in Hegarty (Ed.): *Into the 1990s: the present and future of microcomputers for people with learning difficulties*, Change Publications 1990

  An examination, from a psychological viewpoint, of the kinds of communicative and other activities that some young people are unable to experience, followed by a discussion of how technology might compensate for this.

Microscope, Spring 1995 (Concept Keyboard special)

  Contains a wealth of ideas about using overlay keyboards, including several on basic mathematical understanding.

15 Learners who are bilingual can use multilingual software to help them utilise all their language resources

The use of multilingual software helps to provide access to all languages. It also allows a pupil's knowledge and expertise which may otherwise be hidden or unknown to be shared with others in the group. Pupils for whom English is emerging as a second language may use multilingual wordprocessing to demonstrate literacy in their own language. Learners can make connections between languages as well as recognising and understanding the differences between them. Software such as talking books can be provided in different languages, as can many multimedia titles. Pupils creating their own multimedia material can record their voices in their own language as well as in English, to support both English and other language texts.

Communication between school and home can be facilitated through the use of such software, and it can help parents to become involved in IT work in the classroom. Learning materials and books by new writers can be produced in many different languages, and such work is going on in many multilingual classrooms.

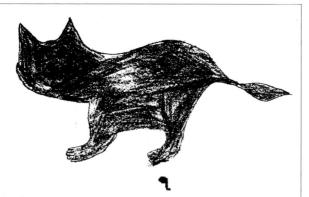

A primary school in Leeds saw a need to create a multimedia application linking pictures, words and speech for the younger Hindi and Urdu speakers in the school.

The application consists of pictures of rooms in a house. When the user points to a door knob another room opens up. In each room there are common items such as tables and chairs. A Year 4 class worked in groups to decide what should be in each room. I selected the most complete ideas to create the pictures of the rooms. The project was announced at the school assembly and Years 5 and 6 were asked to draw and colour pictures of the rooms.

I selected the clearest and brightest pictures and scanned them at the LEA IT Centre. Over the school holidays I put the scanned pictures into the multimedia application and labelled them. Now I am working with Urdu and Hindi-speaking teachers and classroom assistants to organise the recording of speech samples. These will be added to the multimedia files, along with the English versions. We aim to have the application running in the Key Stage 1 area every day for use by both pupils and parents. It will also be used in class as a basis for topic work, and will later be developed by the addition of Bengali, Vietnamese and Chinese.

A college of higher education in Bradford runs a PGCE course for primary teachers. Many of the students are multilingual and this is a strong aspect of the courses offered by the college. Student teachers tell how they worked with multilingual children during teaching practice and helped them use IT to develop further their language skills.

When I gave the children a clue that I could speak their mother tongue, some children spoke to me in Punjabi and Urdu without any hesitation. I did one activity with a 10 year old girl. Her task was to write an imaginary story based on factual information. The story was 'Local homes destroyed by the railways'.

First of all I let her write the story on her own; I wanted to find out about her ability to write in English. When she wrote the story, it did not make any sense. Then I discussed the ideas with her in Punjabi, and then we wrote the story in Urdu on a computer as well. I helped her with the writing in Urdu. She could not believe she could write Urdu on the computer; she was so excited and motivated. It was magic for her: we discussed the story a lot while writing on the computer.

A keyboard overlay

Further reading

Abbott, C.: 'PAL – prolongs active learning' in *Computer Education 78,* November 1994, Computer Education Group

'Parents, Allwrite and Language' was a national project, supported by the Gulbenkian Foundation, which sought to enable young people and their parents to share the first language expertise through the use of multilingual word processing.

Wheatley, V.: 'Word processing in the nursery' in *Developing English: Approaches with IT,* NATE 1993 ISBN 0 901291 33 1

The author describes the use of a multilingual word processor to help children make connections with their language environment and to experiment with their first language using IT.

Edwards, V., and Walker, S.: *Building Bridges: Multilingual Resources for Children,* Multilingual Matters Ltd 1995 ISBN 1 85359 290 0

This book looks at a range of issues, including IT, as they affect UK speakers of the five most common languages apart from English: Bengali, Chinese, Gujarati, Punjabi and Urdu.

IT's English: Accessing English with Computers, NATE 1990 ISBN 0 901291 22 6

This publication looks at how IT can enhance communication and learning in English and the National Curriculum as a whole.

Kemeny, H.: *Talking IT Through,* NCET 1990 ISBN 1 85379 100 8

A discussion document published in conjunction with the National Oracy Project, exploring issues relating to IT and oracy in the classroom.

16 Learners who are experiencing difficulty in reading can be helped by hearing text spoken by the computer

The power of multimedia material allows the creation of information and stories that combine speech, sound, pictures and video with text to present information. Many of these use the potential of CD-ROM to store large amounts of material. As well as factual information provided through encyclopaedia and reference publications, there are a number of talking stories and works of fiction. These range from short animated stories suitable for very young children to well known works such as the novels of Dickens, and Shakespeare plays.

As has been shown over many years with books on tape, many hesitant readers enjoy and benefit from following the text in a book as it is read to them. IT can offer this, plus the considerable extra support offered by the ability to request the re-reading of a particular word or section. Learners can also choose to start reading at any point without having to find the correct place on the tape, and they are also able to hear their favourite parts again and again. The examples opposite show how listening to text being read to them either from prepared material or from their own creation, has helped children learning to read.

Further reading

Hartas, C.: '"Say that again, please" – a reading program using a speaking computer' in Singleton (Ed.): *Computers and Dyslexia,* Dyslexia Computer Resource Centre 1994 ISBN 1 898862 00 1

A report of reading gains by a group of boys with special needs at a school in Gateshead who were given access to structured reading activities with speech input.

Roston, A., et al: 'Hypermedia for the learning disabled' in *Computers and Education,* Vol.22 No.3, Pergamon 1994

A description of the use of hypermedia and speech output with a student who had severe learning difficulties.

Davidson, J., and Noyes, P.: 'Computer-generated speech feedback as support for reading instruction' in Singleton (Ed.): *Computers and Dyslexia,* Dyslexia Computer Resource Centre 1994 ISBN 1 898862 00 1

A research project involving groups of children of different ages in several different schools. The project found marked differences in the value of speech feedback for different children.

A storyboard for one of the talking
books produced for Year 2 pupils

On Monday the greedy clown ate one gorilla.

On Tuesday the greedy clown ate two donkeys.

On Wednesday the greedy clown ate three cows.

On Thursday the greedy clown ate four monkeys.

On Friday the greedy clown ate five dogs.

On Saturday the greedy clown ate six cats.

ON SUNDAY HIS TUMMY BURST LIKE A BALLOON.

A Birmingham inner-city primary school with 96% of pupils of Asian heritage, and situated in an area of high unemployment, identified a need to improve spoken and written English through various initiatives. The children had already enjoyed making books, so it was decided to develop this activity.

We decided to involve a story-teller and a professional children's book illustrator as well as getting the IT support that we needed. We aimed to see that every child made a talking book. We began by looking at existing big books and talked about how they might interest younger children. The story-teller worked with the children on expression, intonation and gestures. She spent three sessions with the children, who then told stories to Year 2, trying out the techniques they had been taught. The children then started drafting their own stories to build on these experiences. After working with the illustrator, the children designed their books and scanned in the pictures they had drawn.

We are only just at the stage of combining sound with text but already it is becoming clear that children have gained considerably from the project. The importance of grammatical correctness became apparent during the story-writing part of the process, and vocal skills were practised in order to achieve the required effect. IT skills were developed as pupils typed, re-drafted and edited text, and as they learned to re-touch their scanned images. A positive outcome has been the enthusiasm and commitment of the children; they have worked extremely hard and, although it has taken some time to get this far, they have not tired of their work.

17 Learners who have difficulty with reading and writing text can use IT-based pictures and symbols

The recent development of sophisticated symbol processing programs has enabled some learners to write more easily, and helped others to read what they have written. As a learner, or an adult helper, types words on the keyboard, corresponding symbols appear above each word. These can be simple pictograms or symbols from some of the well-known languages such as Rebus or Bliss. Some learners can read the symbols where they would never be able to read the words; others can use the pictures to support their reading of the text. New symbols can be added to personalise text and motivate or reward reluctant writers.

Pupils who have difficulty reading can be helped to participate in whole-class activities by using symbol processing software for their writing, because they can have access to the difficult words through graphical images or graphics instead of text. This allows them to explore ideas and express understanding without being limited by their reading difficulties.

Many learners can benefit from the ability of symbol processors to provide a checking device for the correct spelling of a word; this is particularly useful for those learners for whom a spell-checker is not appropriate or helpful. It seems likely that symbol processing will be of use to a much larger group of learners than have used symbolic communication in the past.

A primary school in East London regularly has children arriving in school with no English at all. Although there are classroom assistants who work with these children, talking and reading to them, the computer has proved valuable in providing independent opportunities for listening to and learning the English language.

Children from Years 3 upwards who have recently arrived in this country and who have very little English, listen to talking stories on CD-ROM to give language familiarisation. The fact that they can re-hear any individual words as well as whole passages helps them to make the links between the words and sounds. They also use passages written into an illustrated talking word processor, in which each word is illustrated with a picture or symbol. The reader can hear the whole text in one go or can listen to it sentence by sentence or word by word. These two strategies help with gaining a sense of the language as well as developing vocabulary.

Symbol-supported writing

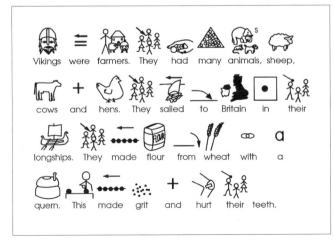

This is a school in Warwickshire for pupils with severe learning difficulties. The school uses symbols as an alternative to text for many pupils who are unable to read standard orthography.

Our children use symbols to complement or as an alternative to text. Recently many pupils were given new freedom to access print. Picture books are, of course very important, but some pupils could not read or produce their own writing until symbol processors became available. We started by helping the children make their own books. We took photographs of everyone and bound these into books, one picture to a page. Some of them talked to their class teacher about what they wanted on their own page next to their photograph. These captions were written in symbol format and pasted into the book. Each picture was covered by a hinged flap to encourage the children to read the symbol text before uncovering the picture to check that they were right.

We also used a video camera to digitise images of each of the children and add these pictures to the program as new symbols. This meant that every time someone's name was typed, their picture would appear on the screen. We are now investigating overlay keyboards and on-screen equivalents so that our children can begin to write for themselves. Some of the children can read easily with the support of symbols, other pupils recognise the photographs and are just learning that symbols carry meaning, but the important factor is that each child has a real book about themselves. They can take these home to read with their parents, just like any other child.

A page from Charlotte's writing book

Further reading

Symbol Users Advisory Group: *Symbols in Practice: Aspects of the use of symbols in learning*, NCET 1993

This booklet contains a series of articles on the use of symbols in educational settings, and discusses the ways in which they can help those who find reading difficult.

Mealing, S., and Yazdani, M.: 'A computer-based iconic language' in Yazdani (Ed.): *Multilingual Multimedia*, Intellect Books 1993 ISBN 1 87151 630 7

A discussion of signs and symbols and the extent to which these are used by Information Technology.

Banes, D., and Coles, C.: *IT for All*, Fulton 1995

This looks at IT in the curriculum for pupils with severe learning difficulties. It includes a section on the use of symbols for writing.

Mealing, S.: 'Talking pictures' in Yazdani (Ed.): *Multilingual Multimedia*, Intellect Books 1993 ISBN 1 87151 630 7

Two investigations of the extent to which the development of symbolic or iconic languages could enable communication without language. Although not concerned with classroom users of symbol processing, these articles provide useful background information.

18 Learners can write more extensively and for longer periods with IT

Some learners experience physical difficulties when writing. Traditional handwriting is accomplished in much the same way, whether the tool in use is a pen, pencil, chalk or a felt-tip pen. The text on a computer screen, on the other hand, can be entered in many different ways, using keyboards, switches, overlay keyboards, speech or other inputs. Since the text, however it is input, is always clear and legible, writers are more likely to continue drafting and redrafting for a longer period. Many writers also find that the act of writing on a keyboard is less tiring than holding a pen. This is often true of learners whose motor difficulties make their handwriting laborious and difficult to interpret.

The ease with which computer text can be read, in comparison with handwriting, makes it easier to return to a piece of work to continue it as well as to redraft or develop it. This will lead to more extensive, longer pieces being produced through word processing than by hand.

The big fight as Frank Bruno steps up to represent England and Britain. Mike Tyson on the other hand is having the time of his life. He's just got out of prison and now has more supporters then Father Christmas. I think Frank Bruno is now as nervus as he's ever been in his life. Mike Tyson had of alredy bieten him years ago.
But there goes the bell oh and Mike Tyson

is piling on the punches into Franks

stomok oh and now his face. This looks like a replay of the last match. The bell

for the end of the first round. Frank Brunos manger giving him a hard time. oh hes got to get up and fight agen. Wap wap wap! Tyson is down and by the looks of things he isnt going to get up ether.

THE END

A piece of work from a reluctant writer

The availability of a large number of portable computers in an inner-city Birmingham primary school enabled much greater individual use of word processing than might usually be possible. All the pupils in the target group had the opportunity to use the portables.

The pupils were very clear about the difference between writing by hand and using the portables:

"I didn't like using computers before. It was hard for me, I didn't know what to do. I enjoy using laptops."

"What I like about laptops are that my hand doesn't get tired and it is fun. I think if I carry on writing on a laptop I will slowly learn how to write fast."

"It's better than handwriting and your hand doesn't get tired."

"I think laptops are better than handwriting because sometimes you get tired when you are writing but you don't get tired on laptops."

Monday 12th December

Views on Laptops

I think laptops are better than handwriting because sometimes you get tired when you are writing but you dont get tired on laptops. They are better than the big computers because you can carry the big computers around you can carry laptops. When you want to save your work you can just press stop and it will save. When you want to get back to your work you just have to press your password which is good. If you have some mistakes you could do spellcheck.

Huma

Further reading

Peacock, M., and Najarian, B.: 'What is important in writing? Some differences in attitude between word-processing and handwriting pupils' in Montieth (Ed.): *Computers and Language,* Intellect Books 1993
ISBN 1 871516 27 7

A research project which shows changes in attitudes to writing on the part of Year 7 and 8 students using word processors, as against the control group who did not have this access.

Hawkridge, D., and Vincent, T.: *Learning Difficulties and Computers*, Jessica Kingsley Publishers 1992
ISBN 1 85302 132 6

The first chapter in this book describes a number of students for whom IT provided greatly improved enjoyment and motivation, provided that software was chosen wisely.

19 Learners who find spelling difficult can benefit from the use of word-processing programs

Technology is the great leveller. Writing is more than laboriously forming letters the right way round and in the right order. A typed passage could have been written by a six year old with poor motor skills or a prolific novelist. No one can make judgements based on the appearance of the work. Instead they look at the content, the style and the message.

Word processors offer more than spell-checking to the learner who finds spelling difficult. The fact that letters and words are displayed clearly and uniformly as they are typed supports the development of visual memory. Teachers will need to ensure that appropriate sizes and styles of typeface are used by learners for this benefit to be realised, but the ability to change these for different learners is a considerable benefit. Many students will also find the ability to change colour combinations on-screen is a considerable help and offers enhanced readability.

Using a word processor a writer can concentrate on building the meaning and sense of the text without worrying about the spelling and punctuation. These elements can be addressed at a second stage, without interrupting the creative flow of ideas.

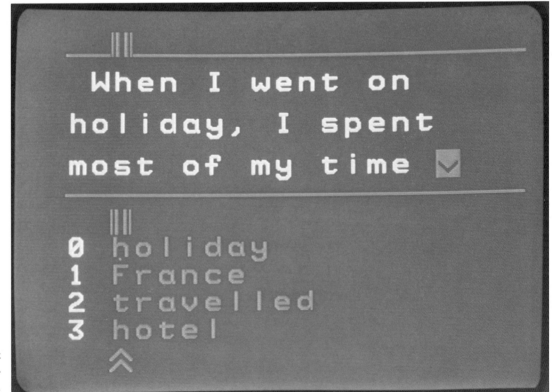

Screens can be set to preferred colour combinations

A basic education class in Nottingham with part-time students uses word processing extensively.

Danny, one of our students, found that using a word processor helped him deal with his spelling difficulties, as well as being useful in several other ways. He describes how he found the program helpful:

"I have difficulty being able to read as I find it hard to see black words on white paper, which is how the majority of words are printed on paper. If I write on paper I have to write it out first, then check for spelling mistakes and then re-write it two or three times. I like using the word processor because I can set the screen to have coloured print, which I find easier to read. I can concentrate on what I want to say and not think about the spelling all the time; I can correct the spelling mistakes later without having to do a complete rewrite. I like the way the final printout looks clean and is easy to read. I feel much more confident about writing since I began using a word processor; it lets me concentrate on my writing skills and helps me write more accurately. Now I take a pride in my work."

Of course, the word processor will not help Danny's handwriting progress, but it will help him improve his writing skills and get more quickly to the stage at which his written communications can be understood by others.

Specific Learning Difficulties - I.T. improves spelling and presentation

I Like   by John

I like history maths Science football and I like making tree houses and swimming and I like going down the brock to my bas and go down the part and I like to play on my computer and my computer games and I like draw pictis of car house and washing the car for my dad and I like going on Holiday to Cornwall and I like play on my bike up and down steets and I like it when get for school so I can woch television and a video I uso like bart shon and robocop.

Word processors can produce more readable writing

Further reading

McKeown, S., (Ed.): *IT Support for Specific Learning Difficulties* NCET 1992 ISBN 1 85379 177 6

McKeown, S.: *IT for Adults with Dyslexia*, NCET 1994 ISBN 1 85379 297 7

These booklets discuss in some detail the particular benefits that word-processing programs can offer to those people with specific learning difficulties.

Day, J.: *A Software Guide for Specific Learning Difficulties*, NCET 1993 ISBN 1 85379 238 1

This publication aims to present teachers and tutors with a range of possible approaches towards using the computer to help pupils with specific learning difficulties.

20 Learners can use IT to help them plan, revise and redraft their writing

It is in the nature of computer-generated text or graphics that elements can be changed, removed or added at any time. Editing, revising and developing a piece of computer writing or drawing, therefore, is often easier than with traditional methods. Something that starts as a sketch or outline can be built upon, parts can be moved or changed and even restored to earlier formats quite easily. This allows the creator to develop a piece of work without fear; to try different expressions or orders of presentation.

It is much easier to rearrange, change and improve text that can be seen than it is to rethink a text which as yet exists only in someone's mind. This is the area in which outlining software – programs which help in the organisation of ideas and structuring of writing – can be very useful. At the same time small-scale but important revisions can be made at every stage of the life of a document.

The ability to change style and layout also adds to the understanding on the part of the learner of the meaning he or she is trying to express. It is much more likely that, in an IT-rich environment, spontaneous writing will be produced as ideas are discussed; these texts are discarded subsequently as understanding progresses and new writing is produced.

Some of the skills are new ones and may need to be overtly taught rather than taken for granted, in which case the teacher supporting the learner will want to be conversant with the techniques themselves. This illustrates the need for teachers to be confident users of IT as well as pupils.

Technology helped pupils plan and build this multimedia story, continually improving it until they were satisfied

A comprehensive school in East Sussex contains a unit for students who are hearing-impaired. The unit is staffed by a full-time qualified teacher of the deaf and a part-time support teacher. The school is in new premises and the Hearing Support centre is purpose-built. The unit decided to investigate the use of various multimedia tools to support the language development of their students.

We use two approaches to language teaching in the unit: aural/oral approaches which involve the maximum use of the child's residual hearing, and the maternal reflexive approach which provides visual reinforcement for spoken and written communication. We also feel that it is important that attention is paid to narrative structure and the writing process as an important area of language teaching. Hearing-impaired people often have difficulties with language, the interpretation of messages and the omission of information.

These teaching methods and the language difficulties of the students link readily with the potential of multimedia authoring tools such as the one used in the project described below. Two students who gained from using the programs were Melanie and Karen, who worked together on *Animal Farm*. Karen has a limited vocabulary and poor syntactical skills, although she is good at spelling. Melanie, her hearing friend in the same class, has a good vocabulary and a fair understanding of how to construct sentences, and is a talented artist. Their skills and difficulties are complementary: they correct each other's mistakes, explain new words and encourage each other. Melanie has also learnt a great deal about the learning difficulties experienced by the hearing-impaired. This work showed us that the use of multimedia IT can be a powerful tool for our students.

Planning a piece of work

```
┌──────────────────────────────┐
│ Israel                       │
└──────────────────────────────┘

┌─────────────────────┐    ┌─────────────────────┐
│ Jewish religion     │    │ * carbohydrates     │
│ dictates diet       │    │                     │
└─────────────────────┘    └─────────────────────┘

┌─────────────────────┐    ┌─────────────────────┐
│ Milk and meat should│    │ Meat has to be      │
│ not be eaten in the │    │ kosher - killed     │
│ same meal.          │    │ according to        │
│                     │    │ religious law       │
└─────────────────────┘    └─────────────────────┘

┌─────────────────────┐
│ Pork and seafood are│
│ forbidden.          │
└─────────────────────┘

        ┌─────────────────────┐
        │ Compare the         │
        │ national dishes of  │
        │ different countries.│
        │ How far does culture│
        │ affect diet?        │
        └─────────────────────┘

┌─────────────────────┐
│ * India             │
└─────────────────────┘

┌─────────────────────┐
│ * China             │
└─────────────────────┘

┌─────────────────────┐
│ * Israel            │
└─────────────────────┘

┌─────────────────────┐
│ * Italy             │
└─────────────────────┘
```

Further reading

Hawkridge, D., and Vincent, T.: 'Writing and spelling' in *Learning Difficulties and Computers*, Jessica Kingsley Publishers 1992 ISBN 1 85302 132 6

Chapter 8: 'Writing and Spelling' provides an overview of many ways in which IT can support learners for whom writing is a difficult or daunting task.

Banes, D.: 'IT for all? The Oldham Micros and Special Needs Exhibition' in *British Journal of Special Education*, Vol.21 No.4, National Association for Special Educational Needs 1994

A useful summary of new developments in the area of writing support.

21 Learners can communicate ideas particularly effectively using multimedia

Young people are skilled readers of multimedia, whether this be through television-watching or a computer screen. For many young writers the opportunity to express ideas in a variety of media, using sound and graphic images as well as text, allows greater freedom and is highly motivating. The use of digitised photographs to illustrate from their own experience or surroundings is very powerful, and choosing and using their own sounds brings the work to life, giving a more personal meaning. Many learners who have access to multimedia are proving to be very sophisticated and skilled authors.

Some learners with special educational needs have been shown to be far more effective writers of multimedia than they are of traditionally-produced texts. IT enables a much wider range of skills and expertise to be tapped, and it is essential that all learners are allowed to demonstrate the full range of their capabilities.

Ellen's picture of herself in her wheelchair

The IT co-ordinator in a primary school in Cornwall used multimedia to enhance children's learning experiences and to encourage the literacy development of children with special needs. The school has 10 computers for 250 pupils, and has recently acquired a scanner and a still video camera.

We were very excited by our new multimedia system when it was placed in my class of 31 Year 6 pupils, four of whom have special needs. I am a firm believer that the computer is a secret weapon that can be used, by any teacher, to zap the most reluctant of pupils into active learning. When our new system arrived I had little idea of how it worked or what precise use could be made of it. I went on an INSET course at a local university and saw the still video camera in use. I was hooked, and I knew exactly how to inspire the rest of my colleagues back at school.

The feature which impressed the class most was the still video camera; seeing an instant photograph of oneself was exciting for both staff and pupils. We decided to build up a class record of events over the term, with Year 6 pupils working in pairs to photograph and write up reports in a class book. They did this with great enthusiasm, using the camera to record visiting speakers and class activities. The resulting printouts provided good evidence of attainment in a variety of National Curriculum areas.

A young fire officer being recorded for the class events diary

We also chose to work with some of our special needs children such as Ellen, who is 11 years old and uses a wheelchair. She has only limited writing ability and a short concentration span; so her activities have to be well-planned and varied. By the afternoon she is tired and very little learning takes place. On some afternoons Ellen visits the nursery where she is accepted by the little ones as a monitor. She also joins in their games, which enhances her own self-esteem and helps her to gain tactile experience and practise social and language skills. Ellen decided she would write her book about the nursery.

Ellen spent a lot of time with her helper deciding on the sequence of events. She then wrote a set of sentences without help, showing a prolonged span of concentration, and drew some pictures of the nursery. It was pleasing to see that she had drawn herself in her wheelchair. We used a multimedia program to put the sentences and scanned pictures together, and then recorded Ellen reading the sentences. As Ellen clicked through the talking book she had made, the rest of the class burst into spontaneous applause: our first talking book had been launched.

Further reading

Dryden, L.M.: 'Literature, student-centred classrooms and hypermedia environments' in Selfe and Hilligoss (Eds.): *Literacy and Computers*, MLA 1994
ISBN 0 87352 580 9

A description of the literacy activities involved in a number of classroom activities in the United States, and some discussion of the potential of multimedia to change the way that classrooms, teachers and learners operate.

Bibby, R.: *The Trojan Horse: exploring texts with IT*, NCET/NATE 1994
ISBN 0 901291 35 8

Contains activities for exploring literary and non-literary texts.

Marcus, S.: 'Multimedia, hypermedia and the teaching of English' in Montieth (Ed.): *Computers and Language*, Intellect Books 1993
ISBN 1 871516 27 7

A highly readable and thought-provoking discussion of this area discussing several different pieces of software and also containing many practical ideas for classroom approaches.

Montieth, M. and R.: 'Using Hypercard in writing narratives' in Montieth (Ed.): *Computers and Language*, Intellect Books 1993
ISBN 1 871516 27 7

Description of a project which looked at the use of Hypercard by three different age groups, and which found the need for new approaches to learning in this area.

22 Learners can be helped to identify spelling and transcription errors in their writing, and to read their own work, by the use of talking word processors

Learners who have difficulty reading their own texts can be supported in this activity by a word processor which can read back to them what they have written. Some learners may need to print out what has been written and follow on this paper version as the computer reads; others may be able to cope with following the text on the screen.

There are many advantages to using speech. It gives instant feedback so that pupils can hear words and make judgements about the spellings. If they type *recieved* it will be pronounced *re–sigh–ved*. The user can hear the mistake. It can also help in those cases where the learner has typed in the wrong word:

I went home and had bacon and eggs for super.

Since *super* is correctly spelt, it would not be picked up by a spell checker but the pupil can hear that it is wrong.

So speech enables the child to identify mistakes which is the first step to improved spelling. The use of speech seems to improve short-term memory and to encourage the development of auditory memory and discrimination which may help with the spellings of individual words. Certainly it increases the learner's independence. They do not have to wait for the teacher to point out all their misspellings.

Speech is not a perfect solution. It cannot help with homophones such as *beech/beach, leant/lent* or with poor spelling which is phonetic such as *Sudenly I felt verry helplus*. Written language is not just spoken language written down, it has different structures and conventions. Speech synthesisers read out exactly what is there and so may sound odd; certainly the use of speech is unlikely to improve syntax. Some learners feel uneasy about their work being read out loud; headphones can provide privacy as well as making life in the classroom more manageable.

Good spellers do not look at the words they are writing or even think about them. They concentrate on what they are trying to say and only look at the spelling at the proof reading stage. For those who are struggling to write, content becomes secondary as they try to break down words into manageable chunks. Spelling needs to be internalised if they are to make progress as writers and speech is one of the many mechanisms which can make this happen.

Hearing text read back as it is written can help the writer to identify some errors as they occur, although the degree to which this is successful will depend upon the quality of the text-to-speech translation. These utilities are improving very fast, and some of the more recent interpreters have very large dictionaries of irregular pronunciations. It is interesting to note that whilst many teachers are reluctant to use text-to-speech synthesis because of the quality of the output, fewer children are bothered. This may be due to the fact that they are used to listening to many different accents and voices on television, particularly in cartoons, so that they become accustomed to doing a certain amount of translation.

It is a particular strength of IT that many tools can be individually set up for each learner, but a prerequisite for this to happen is a developed knowledge on the part of the teacher of the potential of the software.

Teachers involved in the Northamptonshire Talking Computer Project used talking word processors to help their pupils improve their spelling skills.

Talking computers, or more correctly, talking word processors, have been available for some years, however recent developments in the quality of computer speech technology now offer degrees of quite acceptable text-to-speech reproduction. Users of such systems have shown increases in reading ages; spelling ages; short term auditory memory; concentration span; time spent 'on-task', and self confidence and self esteem.

During the project each pupil spent 20 minutes every day over a 4-week period. As well as reading to an adult from a set of prepared cards, the pupil typed sentences into the computer, the words being spoken as they were typed. The particular pattern of reading, listening and writing were determined by each teacher. The teachers reported many improvements:

"All pupils changed in attitude, their concentration sharpened and showed greater focus towards the tasks."
"Pupils got rather clever and were able to 'try' individual letter sounds. The most common were 'b' and 'd'. They listened to the individual sounds and then chose the one they wanted."

A word processor with speech facilities

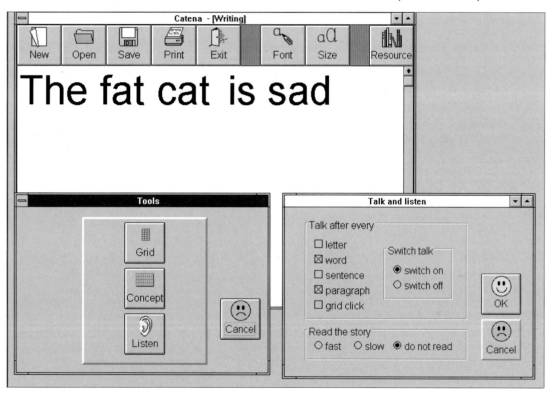

Further reading

Miles, M.: 'The Somerset Talking Computer Project' in Singleton (Ed.): *Computers and Dyslexia*, Dyslexia Computer Resource Centre 1994
ISBN 1 898862 00 1

A description of this well-known project which appears to show real learning gain in relation to the use of word processors which offer speech support.

23 Learners are highly motivated by the quality of presentation of their work made possible by IT

IT can be used to explore different layouts and styles of presentation, and to investigate the relationship between content and presentation. A choice of fonts and sizes, which can convey the style of the piece, as well as flexible layouts, motivates children to take a pride in the presentation of their work. Learners can also examine the relationship between the word and the image in constructing meaning. Many children, starting with 'death by a thousand fonts', soon learn to be discriminating in their choices, and to relate their presentation to that in the press.

Those who are less well-motivated, including young people of school age showing signs of emotional or behavioural disturbance, are often greatly encouraged and boosted by the use of IT to present their work. That is what happened in one East London comprehensive school where ESL pupils produced multimedia texts for younger children.

Further reading

Zvacek, S.: 'Word processing and the teaching of writing' in Hartley (Ed.): *Technology and Writing*, Jessica Kingsley Publishers 1992
ISBN 1 85302 097 4

  An examination of how word processing affects writing, its contribution to motivation and the effect of this on the final product.

Stradling, B., Sims, D., and Jamison, J.: *Portable Computers Pilot Evaluation Summary*, NCET 1994
ISBN 1 85379 301 9

  The section of this report on the 'Impact on Learning' contains a description of the effect on motivation which was noticed during this project.

A multicultural inner-city girls' comprehensive school in London needed to support learners with special educational needs and those who are in the early stages of learning English. The main aim of SEN work in the school is the raising of levels of basic literacy, and the Learning Support Cluster decided to investigate the use of a multimedia authoring package.

We aimed to help some Year 7, 8 and 9 girls produce eight-page illustrated 'books' on-screen and in printed form. We set up a format for this in the multimedia program so that the girls would have the basic structure they needed. The 'books' were at the pupils' level of literacy and stage of English, with the main audiences being infant school children, either English first or second language learners or early stage ESL learners. In addition to writing and illustrating the work, sometimes adding colour after the books had been printed out, pupils recorded the book using the sound facility in the program. In a number of cases, the books were recorded in a language other than English, and on some occasions these languages were used in the text.

We found that using this program was very motivating for our pupils, and the package was also used in full mixed-ability classes by the English Cluster with equal success. Pupils were generally keen to produce a finished product of a high quality, an outcome that is often difficult for them to achieve with paper and pen. They were very quick to learn how to use the package, even the more obscure aspects of the drawing facility. Writing and editing of the text held few problems for them as they were greatly motivated to complete the task.

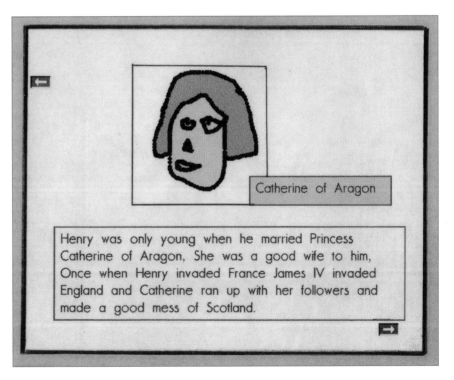

Two versions of the same information produced by a gifted Year 2 pupil at a Cornwall primary school. Dominic has a lively interest in history and shows considerable understanding; access to multimedia authoring has enabled him to present this information more effectively to others.